SandBoaMorphs.com's

East African

Sand Boas

CARE GUIDE

written by:

MARK B. HUNTLEY, esq.

JENNIFER C. HUNTLEY

Copyright & Legal Information

Additional Credits

All Photos Copyright© and credited to: **Jennifer Huntley Photography**

Editing provided by: Michael J. Askew, Esq.

ISBN: 1481003429

ISBN-13: 9781481003421

TABLE OF CONTENTS

INTRODUCTION

What's Covered in this Chapter?

1. General Attributes of East African Sand Boas (Kenyans)
2. This Guide is Specific to East African Sand Boas

Do you own an east African sand boa? Have you been confused by all the conflicting care sheets on the internet? Are you an avid reptile lover and like to keep up on general care of as many species as possible? Have you heard about east African sand boas and are curious if they are a species you can care for? If you answered 'yes' to any of the above, this book was written for you. SandBoaMorphs.com is the leading retailer of sand boas in the United States and we have put together an incredible care guide based on our years of experience with east African sand boas.

We began collecting east African sand boas initially as a way to conquer our irrational fear of snakes. In the process we discovered that the whole family enjoyed their low maintenance care, the ease of handling and their very small size. It has exploded from there! We like this particular breed of snakes because we have a younger family and they are very docile which allows the kids to freely play with them without supervision. These east African sand boas are the very smallest and slowest breed of snake available. There is few pets as easy to own and care for as an east African sand boa whose level of difficulty is perfect for beginners or those short on time. They are the top new species to be collected by reptile enthusiasts due to their incredible attributes, colors and their high number of genetic mutations which has led to new morphs being introduced every year. Simply put, they are THE PERFECT PET FOR YOU!

This care guide is specifically for the proper care of east African sand boas, aka in the pet trade, Kenyan sand boas or Egyptian sand boas, known in the scientific community as Eryx Colubrinus Loveridgei. Generally, you can use the same care for the other sand boa species such as the Indian sand boa, rough scale sand boa, Arabian sand boa, Russian sand boa, Tartar sand boa, Javelin sand boa or the Rosy boa. However, our experience with these other species has been limited to owning only a couple and we recommend you seek out a more experienced breeder or keeper for more specific species care. Throughout this book I will refer to east African Sand Boas as 'sand boas' for simplicity. Please understand that there are multiple species of sand boas and this care guide is specific to east African sand boas, eryx loveridgei.

PHYSICAL CHARACTERISTICS AND SEXING

What's Covered in this Chapter?

1. Size and Weight
2. Dimorphic Sexing
3. Size Differences between Adult Males and Females
4. Differences in Tail Shape
5. How to Sex a Sand Boa by 'Popping'

East African sand boas are a very small, slow, docile and a hardy snake. At birth they range from 4-8" and weigh as little as 3 grams. They are great eaters and will readily take a small baby 'pinky' mouse after their first shed. Sand boas are dimorphic. Di-what? It means that males and females have visual differences that will let you know what sex they are. The most obvious difference between males and females is their size as adults. Male sand boas stay very small and usually range between 12-18" in length as adults and weigh 75-150 grams. Whereas, the adult females grow to a still relatively very small 28-32" in length and will typically weigh 300-500 grams (about ½ pound). If you've owned a sand boa for a few years and are unsure of its sex you should be able to tell simply by its size.

A second difference between males and females is the length and shape of the vent to the tail (the vent is the hole where the waste and babies come out). If you measured a male sand boas vent to tail it should be much longer and skinnier than a females tail which will appear shorter from vent to tail and be thicker. It takes a little more time to be able to use this second indicator effectively but with experience you will easily be able to tell. Keep an eye on the tail!

Sexing your sand boa visually is an effective way to determine males and females but the most commonly used method of sexing a baby sand boa by experienced keepers is 'popping'. I know, it sounds scary and after I describe the process of 'popping' it probably will sound even scarier! Rest assured, if done properly the sand boa will not be harmed. Popping is not something I suggest you 'try' without an experienced person guiding you. Popping is simply, you manipulating the vent to express out the sex organs of the snake by gently applying pressure above the vent while pulling the tail down. If done properly the sex organs will 'pop' out of the vent allowing you to determine if the sand boa is a male or female. Male snakes have what are called 'hemi-penises', yes, as in plural. A male snakes have two penises, one on each side of the expressed vent which appear when gentle pressure is applied. If it is a male you'll see two small red dots on the left and right side of the vent. If you apply additional pressure one or both of the red cylinder like penises will 'pop' out of the snake with each ranging from a few centimeters to ½ an inch long in length depending on the age of the male. Females do not have these and a round lavender colored hole will 'pop' out when you apply gentle pressure to the vent.

Again, I do not suggest you try this without experienced supervision as incorrect popping can result in the death of your snake. If you apply too much pressure the sex organs can become permanently expressed out which leads to infection and death. If you are unsure of the sex of your sand boa you can bring it to a reptile show we attend and we'll sex it for you free of charge. We'll even show you how to 'pop' sand boas if time permits. If we are not in your area you can email **Info@SandBoaMorphs.com** pictures of your sand boas vent to tail and we should be able to sex your sand boa from a picture.

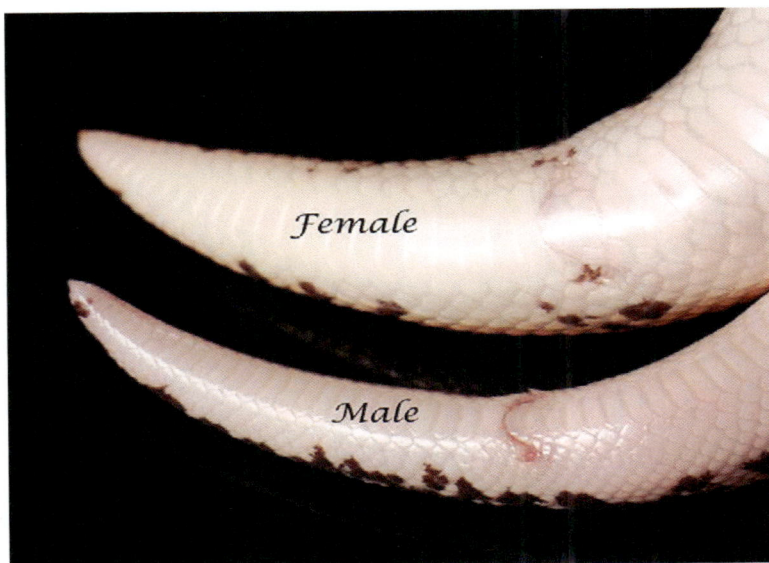

Female

Male

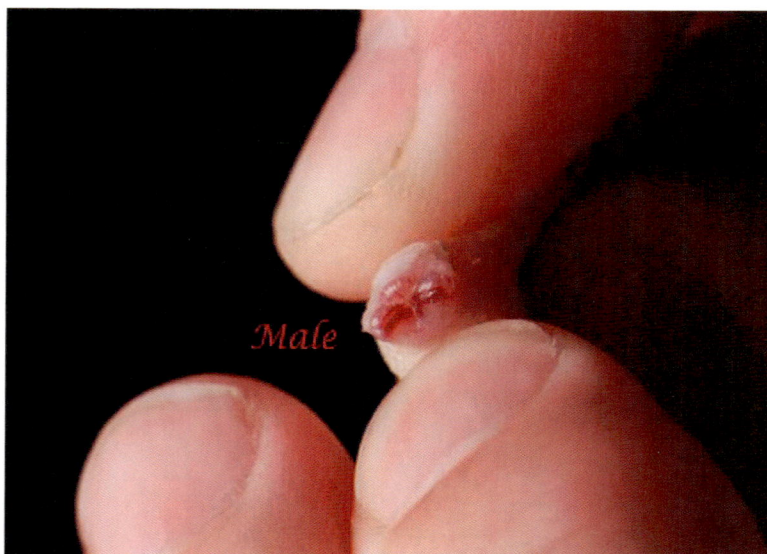

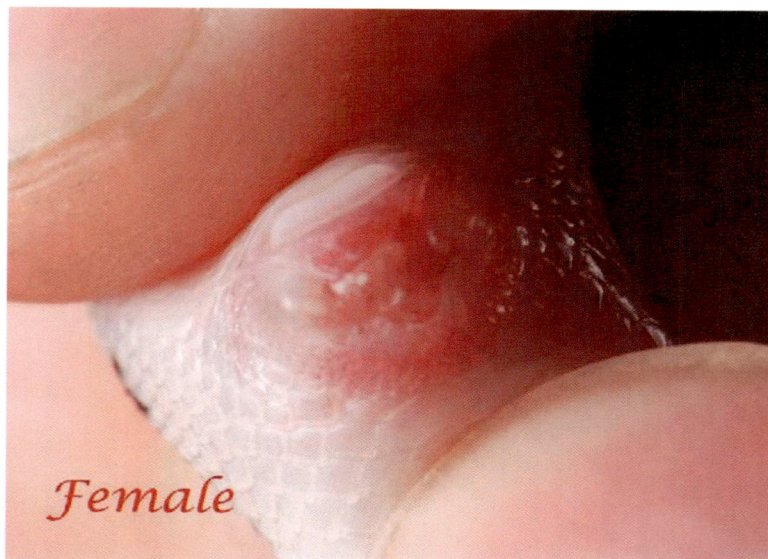

HOUSING AND CAGING

What's Covered in this Chapter?

1. Communal Housing
2. Recommended Aquarium Sizes
3. Recommended Terrariums Sizes
4. Scientific Expression of Sexes
5. Quiz
6. Purchasing at Reptile Shows will Save You Lots of Money
7. How to Find a Reptile Show Near You

Sand boas are very small and docile. They live a very inactive life by choice and thus require minimal space. Sand boas are communal by nature and when housed together will socially interact with one another. As a rule your caging should be long enough that your sand boa can completely stretch out if it desired. For example, if your sand boa is 12" inches long than your caging should be at the least 12" long on one side.

Most sand boa owners house their sand boas in small terrariums, or 10-20 gallon aquariums. These aquarium sizes are typically large enough to house your sand boa for its entire life. Sand boas are communal and do well in colonies so if you are considering breeding or owning multiple sand boas we recommend you purchase a 20 gallon aquarium. We know many people who have successfully housed and bred 1.2 breeding trios in 20 gallon aquariums.

What is a '1.2 breeding trio'? In the scientific world they express the sex of species in numbers separated by decimals for simplicity. The first number in the sequence is the number of males, the second number is the number of females and if there is a third number it indicates that the species is unsexed. For example, 1.2, would indicate one male and two females, whereas 2.4.2 would indicate two males, four females and two unsexed snakes. You try, the answer will be at the end of the book. If I offered to sell you 3.0.2 normal sand boas, what are the sexes and quantities of the normal sand boas I am selling?

You can purchase terrariums and aquariums typically much cheaper at reptile shows than your local pet store, sometimes the savings is as much as 200%! Check with **www.Repticon.com** (one of the largest reptile show promoters in the world) or Reptiles magazine's website **Reptilechannel.com/reptile-events/reptile-events.aspx** to find the reptile shows nearest you.

SUBSTRATE

What's Covered in this Chapter?

1. Sand Boas are Burrowers
2. Loose Substrate Options
3. Substrates that Reportedly have Killed Sand Boas (AVOID!)
4. Proper Use of Substrate
5. Cleaning Substrate

Sand boas are burrowing snakes and require a small amount of loose substrate to help them feel safe. Because of this, reptile carpet and newspaper are not the best choices for substrate. Our top choice is aspen chips aka sani-chips which are finely chopped aspen chipping that our sand boas love and it absorbs waste amazingly well. There are a multitude of other substrates that we have found effective such as, sand, aspen shreds, coconut husks, sani-fresh, and shredded paper to name a few. We strongly recommend against any cedar or pine substrates along with calcium or artificially colored sands as we have received multiple reports of these causing death in sand boas.

Don't make the mistake of overfilling your enclosure with substrate. Substrate's purpose is to make spot cleaning your tank easy and make your sand boa feel safe and secure. We recommend you use only ¼" to ½" of substrate which is plenty to accomplish both of these purposes and allows you to see your snake at all times. If you give your natural burrower sand boa (or any snake for that matter) 2 inches of substrate it is safe to say you will normally just see sand boa noses in the enclosure as they will take advantage of the deep substrate and burrow beneath it. They will be just as happy with ¼" to ½" inch of substrate and you'll be happier because you'll be seeing your sand boa all the time!

WATER AND HUMIDITY

What's Covered in this Chapter?

1. Recommended Water Bowl Size
2. Recommended Humidity Levels
3. Shedding Aids

East African sand boas range along the north eastern countries of Africa from Egypt down into Kenya. Rainfall and humidity in their native habitats are very low. We recommend you use a very small water bowl placed on the opposite end of the heat source in your enclosure so you do not increase the humidity levels beyond 40%. Sand boas will rarely soak and if found in their water bowl it is more likely that they have an inadequate place to hide in the enclosure and are attempting to use their water bowl as a hide. Remedy this situation by adding additional hide boxes to the enclosure. Prolonged exposure to 'wet' environments can and will cause health problems.

Sand Boas do great with the standard home's humidity level, even if you may reside in a humid area (we live in Alabama where it's 100% humidity all summer) your home air conditioner operates by pulling the humidity out of the air and will keep the humidity well within norms for your sand boa. However, when you see your sand boa start to dull in color (sometimes referred to as turning 'blue') it is an indicator that it is about to shed its old skin. This is perfectly normal and is a healthy event that occurs frequently when they are young and less frequent as they slow down growing as they age. When you see your sand boa begin to shed we recommend placing dampened loosely wadded up paper towels inside your sand boas hide box. Keep damp paper towels available to your sand boa until it completely sheds its old skin. We do not recommend that you soak your sand boa in water unless it still has unshed skin after multiple days of attempting to shed.

LIGHTING

What's Covered in this Chapter?

1. Do Not use as Heat Source
2. For Aesthetics Only

Sand boas are nocturnal (meaning they stay hidden during the day and come out at night) and do not require special lighting such as UVB that tortoises or lizards require for proper calcium processing. Any lighting you use should not generate any heat and be for aesthetic and viewing pleasure. We do not recommend overhead heating lights as sand boas do not bask and they greatly increase the overall ambient temperature in the enclosure while inadequately heating the lowest parts of the enclosure where sand boas dwell.

HEATING

What's Covered in this Chapter?

Remember, sand boas are from northeastern Africa where it gets hot! To successfully house any reptile the object is to replicate their environment as best as possible. Inadequate heating is the single largest mistake sand boa owners make. Sand boas require a hot spot temperature (the hottest area in the tank) of 95-105 degrees Fahrenheit. If you are an experienced snake owner but are completely unfamiliar with sand boas this high of a hot spot temperature usually comes as quite a shock. I can't tell you how many times I've been told my sand boa will not eat and it has turned out to be that their hot spot temperature was too low. I do not know of any other snake species that requires such a high hot spot temperature. These are not ball pythons, 88 degrees will keep them alive and comfortable but will not stimulate them to eat.

Why do I have to provide a hotspot? Snakes are cold blooded and require external heat to warm their bodies which stimulates their metabolism and gives them the proper signals that they are hungry and they need to eat. Once they act upon these signals and eat, the heat provides the snake the ability to digest the prey eaten. The single most important action you can take for your sand boa is providing it with the proper hot spot temperature.

In fact, this is probably true for every reptile; the main and most important piece of information is the proper temperature range your reptile should be kept at.

We recommend you provide your sand boa an optimum hot spot temperature with an under tank heater (commonly referred to as UTH). These can be purchased from any pet store and come in appropriate aquarium sizes. The packaging will identify what size aquarium the UTH is recommended for. We recommend you follow the guideline on the packaging and purchase a UTH for your sized aquarium. Again, these can be purchased at significantly discounted prices at reptile shows, typically for $15-20.

Most under tank heaters when plugged directly into a wall will range from 95-120 degrees. The under tank heater should be about $1/3^{rd}$ the size of the entire enclosure and should be placed underneath one side of the tank with the water dish on the opposite side. It is impossible to know how warm your UTH will run once set up. If your UTH is creating a hotspot in your enclosure that is greater than 105 degrees we recommend you purchase a 'Rheostat' at your local pet store to help you regulate the temperature. A rheostat plugs directly into the electrical outlet in your wall but has a dimmer dial between the wall plug and the receiver outlet you plug the UTH into. With this dial you can adjust the temperature of your heating pad and dial it up or down to reach your desired hot spot temperature. Rheostats are relatively inexpensive running around $20.

The ambient temperature, the temperature in your home and more importantly around the water bowl in your aquarium, ideally should be around 76-82 degrees. We find that most enclosures will run within these temperatures in homes that are kept in the 70's year round. If you live in an older house with drafts or like to keep your home cooler you may need to adjust your hot spot temperature up a bit to reach a slightly warmer temperature on the opposite side of the tank.

Sand boas will thermal regulate, slither back and forth from the warmer side of the tank to the cooler side of the tank as they deem necessary, and prefer a thermal gradient between 80 and 100 degrees for optimum health.

How do I know what my hotspot and ambient temperatures are? You will need to purchase a thermometer. There are multiple options but we recommend one of two. First, you can purchase a digital thermometer with a probe attached to it with a wire.

Or the simplest, purchase a digital thermometer sensor that you point at the desired spot and press a button for an instant temperature like magic. The first option with the wire attached to the probe will cost you around $10 dollars and works fine but you will need to move your probe from the hot spot to the other side of the enclosure frequently to ensure that the temperatures are correct. The second option will cost you around $20 dollars but saves you from having to move the probe back and forth and can be used for all of your reptiles or to answer any other temperature curiosities you may have. In any case, you MUST have a thermostat so you can provide your sand boa with the optimum environment.

FEEDING

What's Covered in this Chapter?

1. Birth and First Meal
2. Life Cycle of a Mouse
3. Choosing the Proper Size Mouse to Feed Your Sand Boa
4. Thawing and Feeding a Prekilled and Frozen Mouse
5. Storing Frozen Thawed Mice Safely
6. Feeding Inside Enclosure vs. Separate Feeding Container
7. Feeding Methods and Advice
   a. By Hand
   b. With Feeder Tongs
   c. Drop

8. Consistency is Key
9. Proper Disposal of Uneaten Meals

When your baby sand boa is born they have a bulbous tail which is filled with life sustaining nutrients that they will absorb for the first week or so of their new life. Within ten days after birth they will shed and be ready to take their first meal. Your sand boa will readily take baby pinky mice for its first meal. We find many people are surprised that a new born sand boa can eat a baby pinky mouse which can look large in comparison. Your sand boas jaws unhinge allowing it to eat meals that at first glance appear too big. Even the smallest baby sand boas can eat a day old pinky mouse.

Pinky mice are baby mice that are commonly referred to as 'pinky' due to their hairless pink color. After a week the pinky mouse will have more than doubled in size and will begin to grow hair and this stage of a mices life cycle is referred to as a 'fuzzy'. They will continue to double in size almost on a weekly rate until they reach the 'hopper' stage. At this stage a live 'hopper' ceases nursing and becomes a danger to your snake. The two most significant changes from 'fuzzy' to 'hopper' are the eyes opening and their teeth become fully functional.

We recommend you humanely disable all 'hopper' and 'adult' mice before feeding to your snake. The final stage is adulthood where the mouse becomes sexually mature and look like a typical feeder mouse.

We recommend you feed your sand boa an appropriately sized mouse one time every 7 to 14 days. Whether you are feeding a live mouse or a frozen mouse that has been thawed and warmed (commonly referred to as FT or Frozen Thawed) you must first choose the appropriate sized mouse for your snake. The general rule is not to choose a prey item that is bigger around than your snake. If your sand boa is about as thick as a pencil, choose a baby pinky mouse that is about the same width.

How do I properly store my frozen mice? We store our mice in a dedicated freezer. It use to freak us out to see frozen mice in our home freezer next to the ice cream. Most people have to use their home communal freezer. Here's how we solved that issue. One day I was in the grocery store and saw a bag of brussell sprouts in the frozen food section. Knowing that no one in our family eats brussell sprouts I purchased the bag, threw the green nasty mini cabbages away and stuck my bag of frozen mice inside. I put the mice inside the brussell sprout bag in a gallon size freezer bag and never worried about the mice in the freezer again. Out of sight, out of mind.

How do I properly thaw out my mice? We recommend you fill a designated frozen mice cup with hot tap water and thaw your mice in it for 15-30 minutes. They are ready to feed when they are warm to the touch all the way through. Do not stick frozen mice in the microwave. They will explode. Do not put a cup of water with frozen mice in the microwave. They will still explode. Be sure to properly disinfect everything that comes in contact with both live and pre-killed frozen rodents.

We recommend you feed your sand boa outside of their enclosure. Sand boas are known for being great eaters and your fingers look an awful lot like a small mouse. If you feed inside the enclosure it is highly likely that on a non-feeding day when you reach in to pick up and play with your sand boa it will mistake your fingers for mice and you will receive a feed response strike. To insure that your sand boa does not associate all movement in their tank with feeding you should place them in a small sterilite plastic type tub with the lid firmly fastened and a few air holes melted/drilled into it. Place the snake in the 'feeding tub' with the prey item before you go to bed with a paper towel over the top of them both.

Put the sealed tub back in the enclosure partially on the hot spot, partially off (do not put it completely on the hot spot or you may cook your snake). In the morning release the snake from the tub whether it ate the mouse or not, you'll find most sand boas will have eaten on their own at some point during the night. Flush the mouse down the toilet if the snake did not eat, do not refreeze.

Alternatively, place your sand boa in the tub and pick up the prey item with a pair or feeder tongs (or your fingers). Gently dangle the mouse in front of your sand boas nose while slowly wiggling and bouncing the mouse. This normally will cause a quick strike from your sand boa who will take the mouse from the tongs and begin constricting it. If your sand boa does not strike at the mouse than you will need to take a more active role in enticing it to strike.

If they fail to strike from dangle feeding in front of their nose we move the mouse back to the snake's tail and slowly and gently bounce and tap the snake with the mouse as we work our way from tail to head. Remember we're trying to simulate a mouse walking all over your snake. We will repeat this process until the sand boa raises its head and shows an interest in the mouse. Once your sand boa raises its head you should take the mouse and gently tap the side of the head and neck which usually results in a quick strike. If they do not strike the mouse, we will move the mouse around to their nose and dangle it in front carefully avoiding touching the nose. Sometimes you have to repeat these steps multiple times before your snake will strike.

If after trying these steps a few times without a strike, gently touch the nose of the snake with the mouse. This will cause one of two responses, one response will be that the snake will immediately take interest and move forward and attempt to strike the mouse. If this is the response you receive keep running the mouse along the back and working it back up to the head and nose until the snake strikes. Sometimes the snake will move forward and press its nose against the mouse and you have to hold the mouse gently against the nose until it strikes. Patience is the key.

The second response you will see is the snake recoiling in fear or disinterest. This is typically a 'game over' response and your snake is unlikely to feed this day. This is the reason I do not normally tap the nose of the snake with the mouse until after walking the mouse up the back and tapping the neck multiple times. If your snake recoils, discontinue dangle feeding and drop the mouse in the tank to be left overnight.

Sometimes they are shy eaters and prefer to not be dangle fed and they will eat on their own later that night. Take note of how your snake reacts and repeat the successful methods in the future. Once you have figured out how your snake prefers to be fed we recommend you not mix it up, they are creatures of habit and the more consistent you can keep your feeding schedule and techniques the more success you will have.

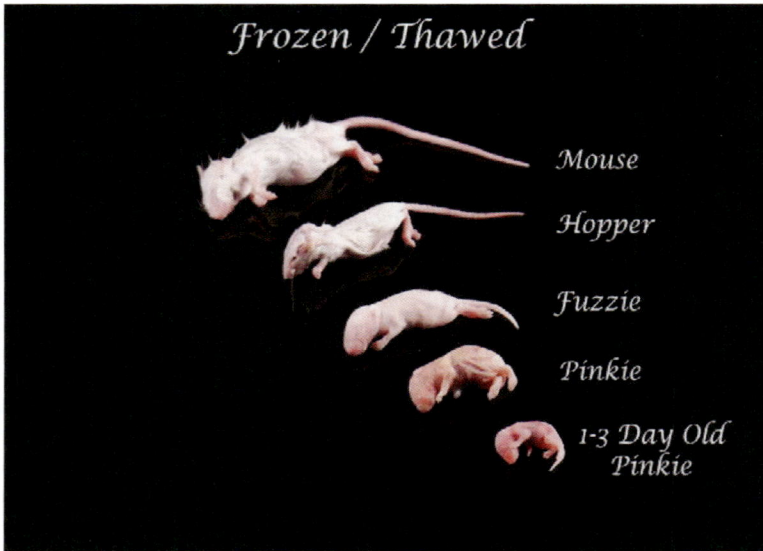

Frozen / Thawed

Mouse
Hopper
Fuzzie
Pinkie
1-3 Day Old Pinkie

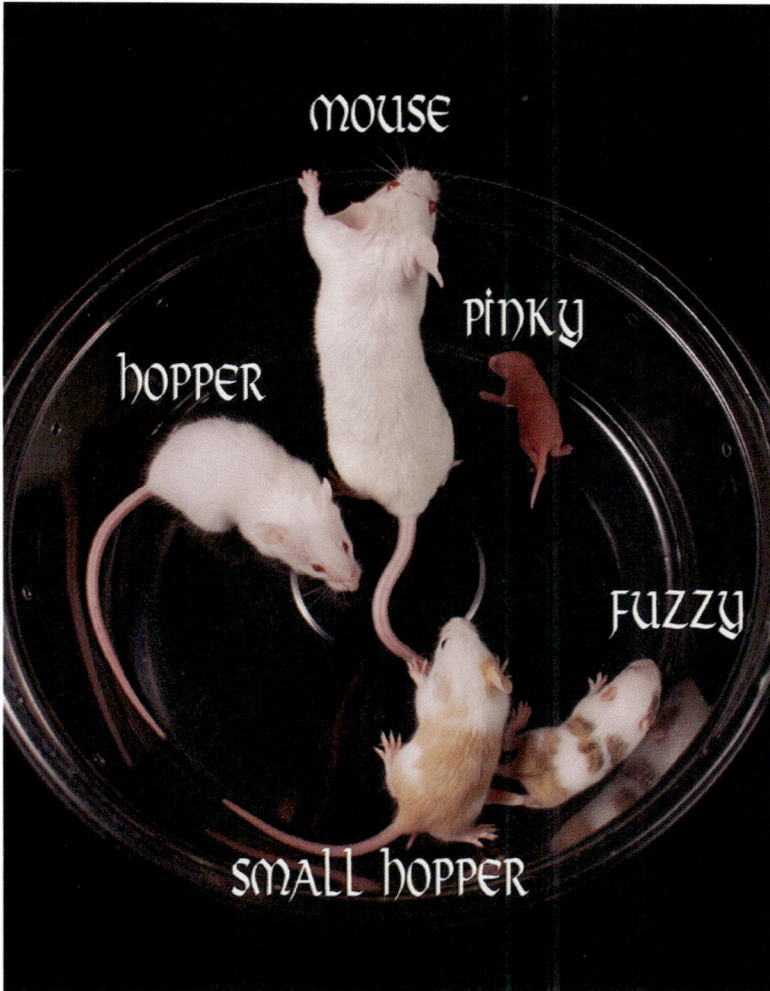

HANDLING

What's Covered in this Chapter?

1. Proper Removal from Enclosure
2. Practical Tips

S and boas are very soft to the touch and are wonderful to handle due to their slow plodding nature and smaller size. They are content to sit in pockets or in your hands with little effort required to control or guide them. To properly pick up a sand boa you should reach into the enclosure and gently pick up their tail with one hand while sliding your other hand along their under belly until you reach near their head. Then gently lift them up out of the enclosure being sure to support their full weight with both hands. Just like you would prefer to not be picked up or held by your head alone, they appreciate the same courtesy.

QUIZ

What's Covered in this Chapter?

1. Answers

Answer to 3.0.2 Question

What are the sexes of the normal sand boas and how many of each?

3.0.2

- 3 Males

- 0 Females (tricky but spot 1 and 2 must have a number even if it is zero, ie 1.0 is 1 male)

- 2 Unsexed

CONCLUSION

What's Covered in this Chapter?

1. Future Sand Boa Guides
2. Our Website Information
3. Our Facebook Information
4. Our Blog Information

We hope you found our abbreviated sand boa care sheet helpful. We will be publishing a much more extensive sandboamorphs.com guide in the coming months. The upcoming book includes a history of sand boas, their legal status, a much more detailed captive care guide, an extensive breeding guide, present genetic morphs including pictures and commentary, the future of sand boas, along with investment opportunities. If you have any questions, concerns or ideas for the upcoming book or changes to this one, please contact **Info@SandBoaMorphs.com**.

For more information about Sand Boas please visit us at:

Website: www.SandBoaMorphs.com

Facebook: www.Facebook.com/SandBoaMorphs

Blog: www.SandBoaMorphs.blogspot.com

QUICK GUIDE TO SAND BOA CARE

What's Covered in this Chapter?

1. Essentials on One Page

Size:
Adult Males 12-18" and 75-150 grams
Adult Females 28-32" and 300-500 grams

Housing:
Small Terrariums
10-20 gallon aquariums
Communal – can be housed together

Substrate:
Aspen Chips, sand, etc.
No cedar, pine, calcium or artificially colored sand

Water:
Provide a small water bowl on opposite side of heat

Humidity:
25-40% humidity
If shedding add damp paper towels

Lighting:
None – only used to better see your snake

Heating:
Hot spot temperature should be 95-105 degrees
Use appropriate sized under tank heating pad
If pad is getting to hot use a Rheostat to regulate the temperature

Feeding:
Feed 1 time every 7 to 14 days
Eat rodents appropriately sized
Majority convert to frozen thawed mice easily

JENNIFER HUNTLEY TALKS ABOUT THE ORIGINS SANDBOAMORPHS.COM

What's Covered in this Chapter?

1. Our Humble Beginnings
2. Our Commitment to Excellence
3. Our Commitment to Customer Service and You
4. The Future of Sandboamorphs.Com

Unlike many in this industry, we did not grow up hunting snakes and keeping them when we were young. In fact, my husband was petrified of snakes which I think makes our story even more compelling. The story begins with our oldest son, Braxton, at a young age being fascinated with snakes. I had grown up in the country in Alabama and had a healthy fascination for snakes but had never pursued this fascination. My husband on the other hand grew up in the 'Big City' and believed 'the only good snake was a dead snake.' Consequently, when Braxton started expressing an interest in snakes it became a major decision as I was all for getting him a snake and my husband was packing his bags and moving out to the barn.

We have owned and bred every type of farm animal and knew from these experiences that preparation for a new species of anything living was key to keeping it living. Our first step took us to Pet Smart where we looked through their offerings of snakes and reptiles and decided on purchasing the 'Best 25 Reptiles as Pets' book.

After reading the book cover to cover on multiple occasions we decided that the sand boas would be the best choice for us based on their size, docile nature, hardiness and generally the universal all around best beginner snake available.

Our first sand boas were ordered online and shipped to our door without any problems. They ate frozen thawed mice as promised and were a great addition to the family. The whole family fell in love with sand boas, including my husband. The family went crazy for sand boas and so we decided to expand our collection by purchasing a couple adult females and males along with focusing on owning a couple of each available morph. Our sand boa holdings quickly swelled to 12 and then more than doubled after an adult female dropped us our first clutch of 20 baby sand boas. We were hooked! Shortly after our first purchase we discovered that the Dixie Reptile Show was located only 45 minutes from our home in Birmingham, Alabama and we began attending the show regularly. Unfortunately, at that time sand boas were not always available at reptile shows and if you did find one or two, they were normally standard 'normals' with the occasional 'anerythristic'. After branching out and visiting the Repticon Columbia and Atlanta reptile shows we started thinking that maybe there was other people like us who LOVED sand boas but could only find them occasionally on the internet. We started vending at the Dixie Reptile Show in Birmingham, Alabama and met a great group of passionate reptile lovers like ourselves, we were not alone! We slowly branched out to other reptile shows including the NARBC, KRE, Dixie Reptile Show and now vend 30-40 Repticon reptile shows a year along with a few others.

Our focus from day one has been on breeding only the top quality sand boas and providing exceptional customer service not only to our clients but to anyone seeking sand boa advice. We have the most diverse collection of sand boas in the country which was acquired by purchasing multiple different sand boa morphs from every serious hobbyist breeder in the USA. Using the knowledge of so many different sand boa morph lines we have continued to stay on top of the latest and greatest morphs but more importantly have stepped back and tried to improve on the most desirable traits of existing morphs. For example, the sand boa is infamous for 'flecking out' (their color can dull or brown with age) but through breeding adults who are 'clean' (not flecked out and have held their color as adults) we have found that 'flecking out' occurs far less often than in the past.

We only breed adults that are 'clean' which translates into exceptional babies for our clients who don't have to worry that one day their incredible looking sand boa baby will lose its color and dull or brown out.

The sand boa is now the newest most sought out species in the reptile industry. This is in a large part due to their very small size, gentle nature and ease of care and high profitability in breeding. At present there are approximately 12 recessive genetic mutations that have been proven countless times along with many of these being bred to one another resulting in visual double genetic morphs such as the snow, snow paradox and albino stripe. We see multiple mutation projects born each year with multiple being proven the last couple years. The sky is truly the limit with all of the new genetic mutations we see popping up across the country and we hope to continue to be on the forefront with the continued humbling support of our wonderful clients and friends.

33987893R00023

Printed in Poland
by Amazon Fulfillment
Poland Sp. z o.o., Wrocław